A LITTLE CHILD
Shall Lead Them

Order this book online at www.trafford.com
or email orders@trafford.com

Most Trafford titles are also available at major online book retailers.

Scripture taken from the King James Version of the Bible.

Print information available on the last page.

ISBN: 978-1-4907-8647-6 (sc)
ISBN: 978-1-4907-8646-9 (e)

Library of Congress Control Number: 2017918886

Our mission is to efficiently provide the world's finest, most comprehensive book publishing service, enabling every author to experience success. To find out how to publish your book, your way, and have it available worldwide, visit us online at www.trafford.com

Any people depicted in stock imagery provided by Thinkstock are models, and such images are being used for illustrative purposes only.
Certain stock imagery © Thinkstock.

Trafford rev. 01/25/2018

Trafford
PUBLISHING® www.trafford.com
North America & international
toll-free: 1 888 232 4444 (USA & Canada)
fax: 812 355 4082

A
LITTLE CHILD
Shall Lead Them

Milagros Flores Santana

Adam and Eve

Adam and Eve
went up the hill
to see about a tree.
Eve was tempted
when the fruit was presented.
Took a bite,
Adam soon followed.

(Genesis 3:1-24 KJV)

Noah Built an Ark

Noah built an ark
Noah built an ark.
It was not easy but,
Noah built an ark.

It was huge.
It was immense and
made of gopher wood.

Noah built an ark
Noah built an ark.
It was not easy but,
Noah built an ark.

All sorts of animals came,
from the tiny worm to the huge
elephant.
Some came by twos, and some by
sevens.

Noah built an ark
Noah built an ark.
It was not easy but,
Noah built an ark.

Noah and his family
made their way in.
The Lord was with them.

Noah built an ark
Noah built an ark.
It was not easy but,
Noah built an ark.

The rain came and
the water rose.
All in the ark were saved.

Noah built an ark
Noah built an ark.
It was not easy but,
Noah built an ark.

(Genesis 6:8–22 KJV)

God Told Abraham

God told Abraham,
"Go forth from the land of your dad."
Abraham obeyed,
and settled in fertile Canaan.

God told Abraham,
"Thou seed shall outnumber the stars."
Abraham listened,
and had several sons.

God Told Abraham,
'Sacrifice your son Isaac."
Abraham complied,
and climbed Mount Moriah.

God told Abraham,
"Do not lay a hand on the boy."
Abraham and Isaac rejoiced.

Abraham the Father of Faith,
obeyed, listened, and complied.

(Genesis 11:31–12:9 and Genesis 22:1–19 KJV)

The Dreamer Joseph

The dreamer Joseph
beloved by his dad.
Shunned by his brothers
when he wore his coat
of many colors.

The dreamer Joseph
was sold into slavery
into the land of Egypt.

The dreamer Joseph
years later
became a great ruler.

The dreamer Joseph
saved his kin
from a great famine,
just as his dreams revealed.
Oh, the dreamer Joseph.

(Genesis 37:1–44 and Genesis 47:13-27 KJV)

Oh, Red Sea

Oh, Red Sea, Red Sea
it parted.
Yes, it parted,
yes indeed.

The Lord led the people
with great power and might.
Then freed Israelites
walked across
and out of sight.

Oh, Red Sea, Red Sea
it parted.
Yes, it parted,
yes indeed.

(Exodus 13:17–14:29 KJV)

Moses and The Ten Commandments

The Ten Commandments
written on stone
by the very finger of the Lord.

Handed to Moses,
who instructed the people
word for word.

The Ten Commandments
written on stone
by the very finger of the Almighty.

Helps us to love,
helps us to live
in perfect harmony.

The Ten Commandments
written on stone
by the very finger of the Lord.

(Exodus 31:18 KJV)

Walls of Jericho

The Israelites marched one by one.
Hurrah!!! Hurrah!!!
The Israelites marched two by two.
Hurrah!!! Hurrah!!!
Walls of Jericho came crashing down.
Hurrah!!! Hurrah!!!

(Joshua 6:20 KJV)

Ruth, Ruth

Ruth, Ruth
was very wise.
She chose to stay
by Naomi's side.

Both were widows.
Both were sad.
Then came a horrible famine
that swept the whole land.

Ruth, Ruth
was very wise.
She chose to stay
by Naomi's side.

Ruth told Naomi,
'Your people will be
my people, and
your God, my God."

Ruth, Ruth
was very wise.
She chose to stay
By Naomi's side.

(Ruth 1:16-17 KJV)

A Shepherd Lad

A shepherd lad
named David,
defeated a giant
named Goliath.

With a sling and a rock.
David slung hard.
Down fell the giant
named Goliath.

Hail! Hail!
Long live the
shepherd lad
named David.

(1 Samuel 17:1–57 KJV)

Old King Solomon

Old King Solomon
was a wise old king,
and a wise old king was he.
Fair and just,
wiser than you and me.

(1 Kings 3:1-15 KJV)

A Lovely Young Maid

There once was a lovely
young maid
young maid
young maid.

Her faith was enormous it
did not fade
did not fade
did not fade.

She advised Naaman when
he became ill
he became ill
be became ill.

'Go and see Elisha the
prophet of God
prophet of God
prophet of God."

Elisha told Naaman, "Bathe in the Jordan
seven times,
seven times
seven times."

Naaman at first
did not obey
did not obey
did not obey.

His servants convinced him to
do as told
do as told
do as told.

When Naaman bathed his
health was restored
health was restored
health was restored.

There once was a lovely
young maid
young maid
young maid.

Her faith was enormous it
did not fade
did not fade
did not fade.

(2 Kings 5:1-19 KJV)

Esther. Esther

Esther, Esther
was a queen.
Esther, Esther
was kind, not mean.

Her famous words
"If I perish, I perish,"
saved her people and
was deeply cherished.

(Esther 4:16 KJV)

Who Was Job?

Who was Job?
A righteous and just man
from the Land of Uz.

Afflicted with pain and sadness,
Job never wavered.

Therefore,
the Lord blessed Job
with peace, health, and gladness.

(Job 2:7-13 KJV)

Daniel

Daniel was nimble,
Daniel was brave.
Daniel survived a night
in the lion's cave.

(Daniel 6:10-23 KJV)

Three Hebrew Boys

Shadrach, Meschach, and Abednego
three Hebrew boys.
King Nebuchadnezzar casted you all
into a fiery furnace.
Not a hair was singed
when the Son of Man
appeared in the midst.

(Daniel 3: 1-30 KJV)

Hush, Baby Jesus

Hush, Baby Jesus
don't You cry,
Mary's going to lay You
in a manger.

Hush, Baby Jesus
don't You cry,
Joseph's going to teach You
how to be a great carpenter.

Hush, Baby Jesus
don't You cry,
You will heal, lead, and teach,
men, women, and little children too.

Hush, Baby Jesus
Don't You cry,
on a cross You will die,
and resurrect on the third day.

Hush, Baby Jesus
don't You cry,
You will be Lord, Savior, and King.
Hallelujah!!! Hallelujah!!!

(Luke 2:1–20 KJV)

Mary

Mary had a baby boy,
baby boy,
baby boy.
Mary had a baby boy,
and named Him
J-E-S-U-S.

She rocked Him
as He slept in a manger,
slept in a manger,
slept in a manger,
and when He stirred
Mary sang Hosannas,
sang Hosannas,
sang Hosannas!!!

Mary had a baby boy,
baby boy,
baby boy.
Mary had a baby boy,
and named Him
J-E-S-U-S

(Luke 1:26-38 KJV)

Peter, Peter

Peter, Peter
walked on water,
'til the waves crashed
then he faltered.
Peter, Peter
cried out,
"Lord, save me!"
Jesus then
extended His hand,
and saved him.
'You of little faith,
why did you doubt?"

Peter, Peter
years later
grateful to be well,
baptized 3,000 souls.
He was commissioned
To tell others
of Jesus'
soon return.

(Matthew 14:22–33 KJV)

Prodigal Son

Prodigal Son, Prodigal Son,
"Where are you going?"
"To see the world", he declared.
Off he went.
He spent and spent and
made some friends,

Until...
no money, no friends, and
thoughts of home and family,
came to mind and heart.
Prodigal Son made his way back home.

His father from a distance
spotted his child.
Ran towards him with open arms.
"My son, my son,
who was once dead is now alive.
Let's celebrate, celebrate."

(Luke 15:11-32 KJV)

Little Zacchaeus

Little Zacchaeus
sat in a tree,
to get a better view
of Him
who died to save us all.

(Luke 19:1-10 KJV)

A Young Lad

A young lad gave all he had,
all he had,
all he had.
A young lad gave all he had
high up on a mountainside.

Jesus smiled and blessed the gift
of five loaves of barley,
and two small fish.

Then...

Jesus fed a multitude,
a multitude,
a multitude.
Jesus fed a multitude
high up on a mountainside.

The crowd then
ate and ate,
ate and ate.
The crowd ate and ate,
high up on a mountainside.

(John 6:1–14 KJV)

Printed in the United States
By Bookmasters